PARENT-TEACHER COLLECTION

Learn with Me: Crafts & Gifts

Carson-Dellosa Publishing LLC
Greensboro, North Carolina

Note that some activities in this book may present safety issues. Before beginning the activities, ask families' permission and inquire about the following:
- Children's food allergies and religious or other food restrictions
- Possible latex allergies
- Children's scent sensitivities and/or allergies
- Children's plant and animal allergies

Also remember:
- Uninflated or popped balloons may present a choking hazard.
- Magnets and small pieces containing magnets should be kept away from young children who might mistakenly or intentionally swallow them. Seek immediate medical attention if you suspect a child may have swallowed a magnet.
- Exercise activities may require adult supervision. Children should always warm up prior to beginning any exercise activity and should stop immediately if they feel any discomfort during exercise.
- All children's families are different. Before beginning any family activity, review the activity cards and remove any that could cause sensitivity issues.

Credits

Content Editor: Joanie Oliphant

Copy Editor: Sandra Ogle

Layout Design: Lori Jackson

Spectrum
An imprint of Carson-Dellosa Publishing LLC
PO Box 35665
Greensboro, NC 27425 USA
www.carsondellosa.com

ISBN 978-1-936024-78-0
335107811

Table of Contents

Introduction

Welcome to *Learn with Me: Crafts & Gifts.* While working on the activities in this book, you and your child will spend quality time having fun together. Just as important, your child will be practicing important skills. Research tells us that following directions and performing fine motor activities, such as drawing, cutting with scissors, gluing, and manipulating small objects, are important preschool skills. Your child will be building valuable kindergarten readiness skills while having fun and enjoying your time together.

Each activity in this book has been designed with step-by-step directions and will result in a craft to play with, display, or give to a special person as a gift. Some of the crafts and gifts will take just a few minutes to create. The Painted Bubble-Saurus is quick and easy. (See page 36.) Other activities take a little longer, such as the Orange Pomander Ball. (See page 25.) Plan to work on this activity and activities like this for a little while each day for several days. With such projects, children build the ability to persevere and learn that it can take some time to create wonderful things. Your child's mood, attention span, and personal interests may change from day to day. Be aware of these factors when choosing an activity and be prepared to put a project aside if your child loses interest.

For your convenience, a list of recommended supplies and materials has been provided on pages 5 and 6. Many projects are made with common household items, such as disposable foam bowls and paper plates. Basic school supplies, including glue, crayons, markers, and scissors, are used throughout. Some projects are made from pinecones and other natural objects that you and your child can collect together. You may wish to purchase some craft items such as pom-poms and colorful feathers. Look for ways to use things you already have around the house. For example, do you have a jigsaw puzzle that is missing some pieces? Use the pieces you have to make attractive jewelry for gifts. (See page 61.) We encourage you to involve your child in gathering the materials before beginning an activity.

As you work together, focus on having fun and on the excitement your child feels upon completing a project. Help your child find places to display the creations and allow time for playing with the toys. Be responsive to, "Let's make another one!" Repetition is a natural way for children to practice skills. You will be spending your time in the valuable pursuit of fine motor development and other important skills that will help prepare your child for kindergarten and beyond.

Enjoy Learning Together!

The Spectrum Team

Recommended Supplies and Materials

The following is a list of some of the materials used in the activities in this book. You will find that many of them can be found around the house. Others can be purchased at discount stores, craft stores, or office supply stores. Once you and your child have chosen an activity to work on together, we encourage you to involve your child in gathering the needed supplies.

Craft Supplies:

Card stock
Chenille stems
Craft feathers
Doilies
Fabric scraps
Felt scraps
Glitter and glitter glue
Googly eyes (wiggle eyes)
Jewelry bar pins
Magnetic strip tape
Patterned paper (scrapbook paper)
Plastic sewing needles
Pom-poms
Ribbon
Sequins
Tissue paper
Wooden craft sticks
Yarn

School Supplies:

Brass paper fasteners
Clear tape
Construction paper
Crayons
Glue sticks
Hole punch
Large mailing envelope
Markers

Paint (acrylic, tempera, or watercolor)
Paintbrushes
Paper clips
Pencils
Rubber bands
Stapler
White glue

Household Supplies:

Aluminum foil
Applesauce
Bubble packaging material
Buttons
Candles (used)
Caps from bottles and jars (clean and dry)
Cardboard tubes (foil, plastic wrap, gift wrap, etc.)
Cereal boxes (empty and clean)
Cinnamon
Clothespins (wooden)
Clothing hangers
Cookie cutters
Cornstarch
Corn syrup
Family photographs
Flour
Disposable foam bowls
Disposable foam plates
Disposable foam sponges

Recommended Supplies and Materials

Food coloring
Magazines
Nails
Newspaper
Oranges
Paper bags
Paper bowls
Paper plates
Paper towels
Pasta, popcorn, or rice (uncooked)
Plastic water or soft drink bottles (empty, clean, and dry)
Puzzles pieces
Salt
Straws
Toothpicks
Waxed paper
Whole cloves

Utensils:

Baking sheet
Basting brush
Measuring cups and spoons
Mixing bowls
Rolling pin
Scissors
Wooden or plastic spoons

Natural Items:

Acorns
Birdseed
Cedar bark or shavings
Pinecones and pine needles

Cookie-Cutter Stained Glass

Materials:
- Aluminum foil (approximately 8" x 8" [20 cm x 20 cm])
- Newspaper or old magazine
- Cookie cutters
- Pencil
- Glue stick
- Tissue paper scraps in a variety of colors

Directions: With adult help...

1. Put the aluminum foil on the newspaper.

2. Press a cookie cutter into the aluminum foil hard enough to mark the cookie cutter's outline.

3. Trace the outline with the pencil. Press hard enough to cut the cookie cutter's outline.

4. Carefully remove the shape, leaving its space in the foil.

5. Repeat the process to make three or four shapes in the foil.

6. Put glue around the cut out spaces in the foil.

7. Put scraps of colored tissue paper over the holes.

8. Tape your cookie-cutter stained glass picture on a window.

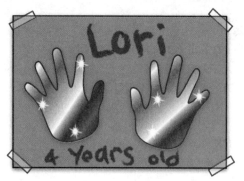

Materials:
- Scissors
- Aluminum foil
- Pot holder or old magazine
- Ballpoint pen
- Glue stick
- Construction paper
- Crayon or marker

Directions: With adult help...

1. Cut two pieces of aluminum foil about 1" (2.5 cm) bigger than your hands.

2. Put the pot holder or magazine on a flat surface. Put one piece of foil on the pot holder.

3. Put one hand on the foil. Spread out your fingers.

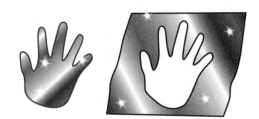

4. Ask an adult to slowly draw around your hand with a pen. He should press the pen down hard enough so that it tears the foil under his fingers.

5. Tear away the extra foil leaving only your handprint. Put the print aside.

6. Repeat the process to make a print of your other hand.

7. Glue the handprints to a piece of construction paper.

8. Write your name and age on the paper.

Paper Bead Necklace

Materials:
- Clear tape
- 1" x 3" (2.5 cm x 7.6 cm) strips of colorful paper
- Wooden spoon with long handle
- 30" (76 cm) of yarn

Directions: With adult help...

1. Tear lengths of clear tape (approximately 1" [2.5 cm]). Stick lengths of tape to the edge of a table so that they will be ready to use.

2. Roll a strip of paper around the spoon handle.

3. Hold the strip in place while an adult puts tape on the paper strip to keep it in a loop.

4. Slide the paper "bead" off the spoon handle. Set it aside.

5. Repeat steps 2 through 4 until you have all of the beads you want.

6. String the beads on the yarn.

7. Adjust the length of the yarn so that it fits over your head. Tie the ends securely.

People I Love Paper Chain

Materials:
- Marker
- Eight 1" x 11" (2.5 cm x 28 cm) strips of paper (Any lightweight paper will work. For best results, use paper with colorful designs, such as scrapbook paper.)
- Glue stick

Directions: With adult help...

1. Write the name of someone you love on each paper strip.

2. Form one strip into a circle with the writing on the outside.

3. Overlap the ends of the loop. Glue the ends together.

4. Place the next strip through the first circle. Glue the ends together.

5. Repeat step 4 until you have used all of the paper strips.

6. Hang the chain in an easy-to-reach place. Create more paper strips as you think of more people you want to add to your chain.

Note: You can also make paper chains to count down days until an important event. Use a calendar to count how many days you have to wait. Make a chain with that number of loops. Take one loop off every day until the event arrives.

Materials:
- Scissors
- Pinwheel pattern (below)
- Hole punch
- Pencil
- Wide straw
- Glue stick
- Brass paper fastener

Directions: With adult help...

1. Cut out the pattern. Cut the slashed lines at each corner of the square.
2. Punch a hole in each corner on the X.
3. Punch a hole with a pencil on the O in the center.
4. Punch a hole in the straw with a hole punch.
5. Bend each corner with a hole. Glue it to the center of the pinwheel over the hole you punched on the O.
6. Place the flat side of the pinwheel against the straw. Line up the center hole with the straw's hole.
7. Insert the brass paper fastener through the pinwheel and straw. Bend back the "wings" of the fastener to hold it in place. (If your pinwheel will not spin, loosen the fastener.)
8. To play with the pinwheel, grasp the straw near the bottom and blow air into the paper loops of the pinwheel.

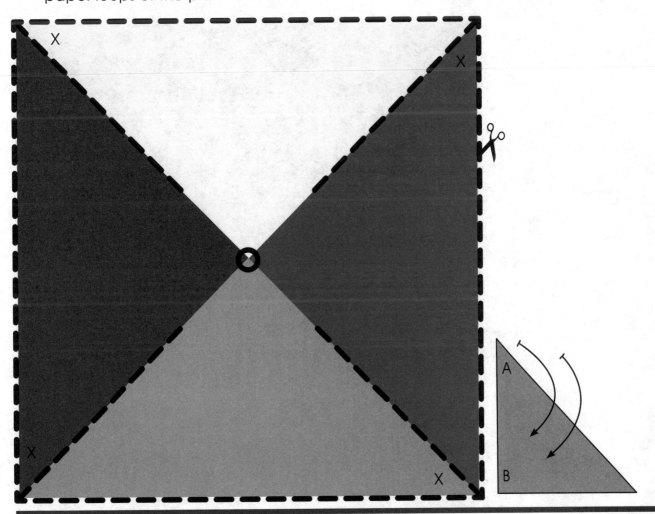

Snowstorm in My Window

Materials:
- Paper lace doilies (Doilies that are 4" to 8" (10 cm to 20 cm) in diameter fit best in most windows.)
- Scissors
- Hole punch
- White yarn or narrow ribbon
- Spray starch
- Iron

Directions: With adult help...

1. Fold the doily in half. Align the edges. Fold it in half two more times.

2. Cut square, triangle, and rectangle shapes into the edges of the folded doily. Be careful not to cut any of the edges off completely, or your snowflake will fall apart.

3. Carefully open the doily and reveal a snowflake!

4. Make four or five more snowflakes.

5. Punch a hole near the edge of each snowflake. Attach yarn or ribbon to hang up your snowflake.

6. To strengthen a large snowflake, spray it with starch and iron it with a warm iron.

7. Hang the snowflakes in a window.

Note: If you do not have paper doilies, you can make snowflakes from circles of paper. Trace round dinner plates, dessert plates, or cereal bowls to make different sizes of circles.

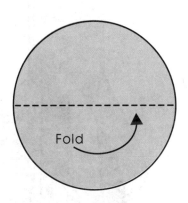

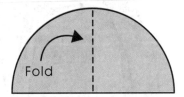

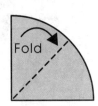

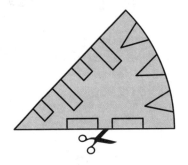

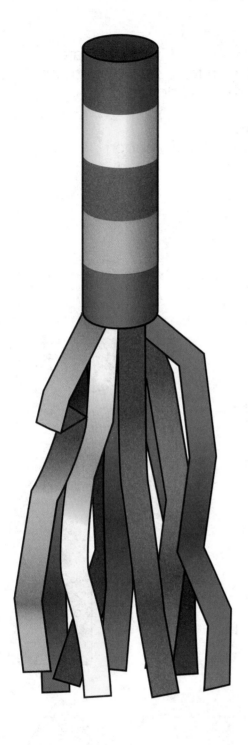

Materials:
• Scissors
• 1" (2.5 cm) strips of tissue paper in a variety of colors
• 5" (12.7 cm) cardboard tube (Tubes from plastic or aluminum wrap work best.)
• Glue stick

Directions: With adult help...

1. Cut one 1" x 20" (2.5 cm x 50.8 cm) strip of each of the colors of tissue paper.

2. Cut the strips in half lengthwise.

3. Cover the outside of the cardboard tube with glue.

4. Wrap half of the tissue paper strips around the tube. Glue the ends of the tissue paper together.

5. Cover about ½" (1.25 cm) of the inside edge of the tube with glue.

6. Attach the remaining strips to the inside edge of the tube.

7. Hang the wind sock near an open door or window. The breeze will make the tissue paper strips move.

Note: You can hang the wind sock outside as long as it stays out of the rain.

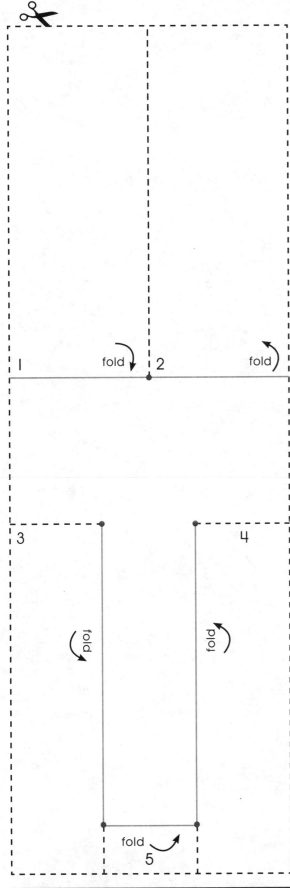

	fold ↓	2	fold ⤴
1			

3   fold ↓   fold ↑   4

fold ⤴
5

Materials:
- Scissors
- Helicopter pattern (left)
- Paper clip

Directions: With adult help…

1. Cut out the helicopter along the outside edge.
2. Cut along the slashed lines. Be sure to stop cutting at each red dot.
3. Fold the paper strip with the 1 toward you along the blue line.
4. Fold the paper strip with the 2 away from you along the blue line.
5. Fold the paper strip with the 3 across the center space.
6. Fold the paper strip with the 4 across the center space. It will overlap 3.
7. Fold the paper strip with the 5 upward. Connect it to the folded 3 and 4 strips with a paper clip.
8. To fly your helicopter, hold it high in the air, let go of it, and watch it spin to the floor or ground.

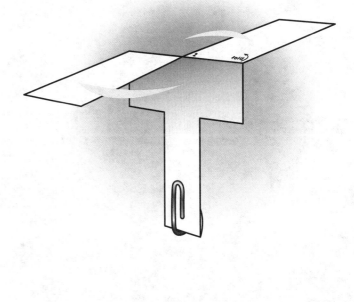

Sun, Moon, and Stars Mobile

Materials:
- Yellow crayon, marker, or paint
- Two 6" (15.25 cm) paper plates
- One 8" (20.3 cm) paper plate
- Star-shaped cookie cutter
- Scissors
- White glue and glitter (optional)
- Hole punch
- Ribbon or yarn
- Small plastic clothing hanger

Directions: With adult help...

1. Color or paint both sides of the small paper plates yellow. Color both sides of the large paper plate's flat center yellow.

2. Make short cuts all of the way around the edge of one small paper plate.

3. Bend the tabs made from the cuts toward the center of the plate.

4. Draw a crescent moon shape on one small paper plate. Cut it out.

5. Trace a star-shaped cookie cutter three times on the large paper plate. Cut them out.

6. If desired, cover the shapes with glue and sprinkle them with gold or silver glitter.

7. Punch a hole near the edge of each shape. Thread ribbon or yarn through the hole and tie a knot.

8. Tie the loose end of the yarn to the hanger.

9. Display the mobile in your room.

Materials:
- One 8" x 10" (20.3 cm x 25.4 cm) sheet of cardboard (The front and back sides of cereal boxes work well.)
- Glue stick
- Full-page picture from a magazine
- Scissors
- Large mailing envelope

Directions: With adult help...

1. Cover the cardboard with glue. Place the magazine picture on the cardboard. Rub the whole picture to flatten and stick it all of the way to the edges.

2. Allow the glue to dry.

3. Cut the cardboard into six to nine puzzle pieces.

4. Store the puzzle pieces in a large mailing envelope when you are not playing with them.

My Family Tree

Materials:
- Construction paper
- Glue stick
- 8" (20.3 cm) paper plate
- Scissors
- Family photographs (If you do not have photographs, you can draw the members of your family.)

Directions: With adult help...

1. Make a tree out of construction paper.

2. Glue the tree to a paper plate.

3. Trim the photographs so that they will all fit on the tree.

4. Glue a photograph of yourself in the middle of the tree.

5. Glue photographs of your family members around the plate.

6. As you glue, discuss how each person is related to you and the rest of your family members.

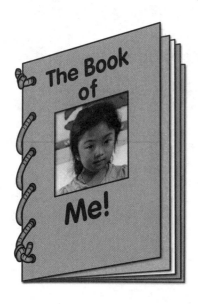

Materials:
- Construction paper in a variety of colors (5 or more sheets)
- 3" (7.6 cm) circle and 3" square templates cut from construction paper
- Scissors
- Photographs 4" x 4" (10 cm x 10 cm) or larger (Choose pictures showing you at different ages, in different moods, and doing different activities.)
- Clear tape
- Markers
- Paper clip
- Thick yarn

Directions: With adult help…

1. Fold each sheet of construction paper in half.

2. Open the paper. On the left side of the fold, trace a 3" (7.6 cm) circle or square near the middle of the page.

3. Cut out the circle or square shape.

4. Place one of your photographs facedown over the shape. Tape it to the construction paper on all four sides.

5. Repeat this process for each photograph.

6. Tell an adult about each picture. Have the adult write what you say under the picture.

7. To protect the pages, tape the three open edges of each page.

8. When all of the pages are finished, punch six holes along the folded edge of the first page.

9. Using the first page as a template, punch holes in each page of your book. The holes must be directly on top of each other. To do this, punch holes in the first page. Line up each page in turn and punch through the same holes again.

10. To bind the book, line up the pages and holes. Use a paper clip to hold them together.

11. Thread the yarn down into the first hole. Bring the yarn around the book's edge to thread it through the second hole. Weave the yarn in and out through all of the holes.

12. Tie a knot at each end to hold the yarn in place.

Materials:
- White glue
- Fabric circle, 5" (12.7 cm) in diameter
- Cap from baby food jar (or a cap from a jelly jar)
- 12 to 15 tiny pinecones, acorn caps, or large seeds
- Glitter glue (optional)
- 1" (2.5 cm) length of magnetic strip tape

Directions: With adult help…

1. Glue the fabric, right side up, to the inside of the jar cap.

2. Squeeze a puddle of glue into the cap on the fabric.

3. Place the pinecones, acorn caps, or seeds in the glue puddle.

4. Allow the glue to dry completely.

5. If desired, decorate your project with glitter glue.

6. Trim the edges of the fabric to about an inch around the cap.

7. Secure the magnetic strip to the back of the cap.

8. Display your magnet on the refrigerator.

Safety First! (See page 2.)

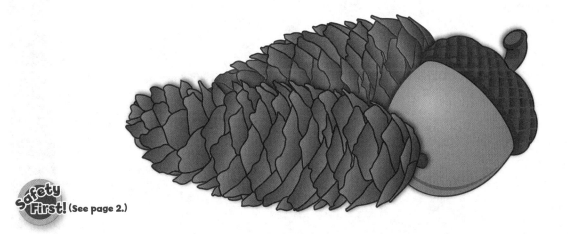

Pinecone Bird Feeder

Materials:
- Chenille stem
- Pinecone
- Newspaper
- Basting brush
- Light corn syrup
- Birdseed
- Yarn or ribbon

Directions: With adult help...

1. Wrap the chenille stem tightly around the pinecone. Make a small loop with the chenille stem ends at the top of the pinecone.

2. Place the pinecone on several layers of newspaper. (Tip: It is best to do the next steps outdoors.)

3. Using the basting brush, paint the pinecone with corn syrup.

4. Sprinkle birdseed onto the corn syrup. Allow the corn syrup to dry completely.

5. Tie a piece of yarn or ribbon through the loop on the chenille stem.

6. Hang the feeder outside to attract birds.

 **(See page 2.)**

Ingredients:
- ¼ cup ground cinnamon
- 1 tablespoon all-purpose flour
- ¼ cup applesauce

Materials:
- Waxed paper
- Rolling pin
- Cookie cutters, various shapes
- Straw
- Baking sheet
- Spatula
- Oven
- Acrylic or tempera paint (any color)
- 12" x ¼" (30.5 cm x 0.65 cm) ribbon (one for each hang-up)

Directions: With adult help…

1. Mix the cinnamon, flour, and applesauce together to form a smooth dough.

2. Sprinkle one sheet of waxed paper with a little extra flour. Roll dough between two sheets of waxed paper to ¼" (0.65 cm) thick.

3. Remove the top sheet of paper. Cut out shapes from the dough with cookie cutters.

4. Make a hole in the top of each cutout using a straw.

5. Place the cutouts on a baking sheet using a spatula. Bake them in an oven at 150°F (65°C) for one hour or until thoroughly dry.

6. Let the cutouts cool completely. Remove them from the baking sheet. If desired, paint them with acrylic paint.

7. After the paint dries, thread a ribbon through the top hole of each cutout. Tie the ribbons into secure bows, leaving room to hang the cutouts.

 **(See page 2.)**

Potpourri Pouch

Materials:
Assorted dry, natural items:
- Cedar leaves, bark, and/or shavings
- Acorns
- Dried clover heads
- Small pinecones
- Pine needles
- Bay leaves
- Cinnamon sticks
- Lunch-size paper bag
- Cinnamon oil
- 8" x 8" (20.3 cm x 20.3 cm) fabric square
- Pinking shears or regular scissors
- Ribbon

Directions: With adult help...

1. Place cedar leaves, bark, and/or shavings; acorns; clover heads; pinecones and pine needles; bay leaves; and cinnamon sticks in a paper bag. Leave at least 4" (10 cm) of room at the top of the bag.

2. Put three drops of cinnamon oil in the bag.

3. While holding the bag closed, shake it vigorously at least 12 times.

4. Pink the edges of the fabric square using the shears.

5. Place a mound of the potpourri mixture in the center of the fabric square.

6. Pull the fabric square corners up. Tie them securely closed with the ribbon. (A pinecone tied into the bow helps make an attractive gift.)

Safety First! (See page 2.)

Materials:
- Sturdy toothpicks
- One firm, ripe orange
- Whole cloves
- Nail
- Ribbon

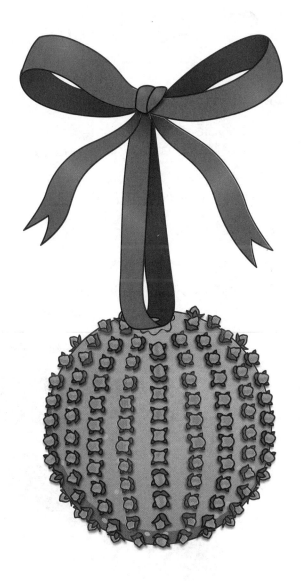

Directions: With adult help...

1. Using a toothpick, poke holes all over the orange's skin.

2. Push a whole clove into each hole. (Place the cloves as close as possible to cover the orange completely.)

3. Tie a ribbon around a nail close to the head.

4. Push the nail and ribbon into the top of the orange.

5. Hang the orange in a dry, cool place for two to three weeks until fully dry.

6. Give it to a special person as a gift to place in a drawer or closet to give off a pleasant odor.

 **(See page 2.)**

Materials:

- Two sheets of construction paper, one larger than the other
- Used white candle or white crayon
- Large paintbrush
- Watercolor paints

Directions: With adult help…

1. Scribble or draw on the smaller piece of construction paper using the candle as you would a crayon or marker. For best results, press hard with the candle.

2. Paint the paper with watercolor paints. The paint will color the paper, but it will not cover the candle wax.

3. Watch your candle drawing appear!

4. Allow the artwork to dry.

5. Frame it by gluing the art to the larger sheet of construction paper.

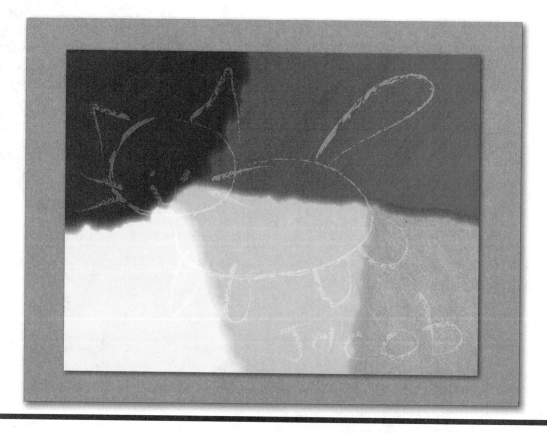

Frosted Winter Scene

Ingredients:
- ¼ cup salt
- ¼ cup boiling water

Materials:
- Scissors
- Construction paper scraps
- Construction paper (whole sheet)
- Glue stick
- Paintbrush
- Salt mixture

Directions: With adult help...

1. Mix the salt and boiling water. Let the mixture cool before you start the project.

2. While you wait, cut out evergreen trees and other shapes, such as animals or a house, for your picture.

3. Glue the trees and other shapes to the construction paper. Allow the glue to dry.

4. Use the brush to paint the salt mixture over the whole picture. Allow it to dry.

5. Look at your picture. You will see that it is covered with frosty crystals.

 **(See page 2.)**

Sponge Painters

Materials:
- Permanent marker
- Disposable foam sponges
- Scissors
- Wooden craft sticks
- White glue
- Paper plate
- Paper towel

Use the sponge painters with the activity on page 29.

Directions: With adult help...

1. Using a permanent marker, draw the outlines of several shapes on the sponge.

2. Cut out the shapes.

3. Cut a small slit in the middle of each shape.

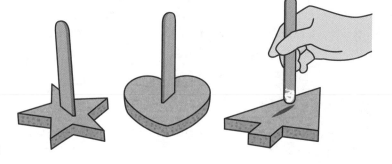

4. Cover the tips of the wooden craft sticks with glue. Slide them into the slits in the sponges. Allow the glue to dry.

5. To use your sponge painters, pour some paint on a paper plate. Gently dip the sponge into the paint. Tap it lightly on a folded paper towel to remove some of the paint. Use it like a stamp to paint shapes on paper.

Sponge-Painted Masterpiece

Materials:
- Paper towel
- 8" (20.3 cm) paper or disposable foam plate
- Acrylic or tempera paint, any color
- Sponge painters (page 28), any shape
- 9" x 12" (23 cm x 30.5 cm) construction paper
- Glue stick
- 11" x 14" (28 cm x 35.6 cm) sheet of paper (This will be used to frame your masterpiece.)

Directions: With adult help...

1. Place a folded paper towel on an 8" (20.3 cm) paper or disposable foam plate.

2. Pour small puddles of paint on the paper towel. Use as many colors as you like.

3. Dip the sponge painter in the paint. Press the sponge painter all over your paper.

4. Switch to another sponge painter and/or color. Continue to paint until the construction paper is completely covered. Allow the paint to dry.

5. Frame your sponge-painted masterpiece by gluing it to the center of a large sheet of paper.

My Name Door Hanger

Materials:
- Letter stencils on pages 31 and 33 for the letters in your first name
- 4 ½" x 12" (11.4 cm x 30.5 cm) sheet of construction paper, any color
- Glue stick
- Sponge or sponge painter (page 28, circle or square)
- Acrylic or tempera paint, any color
- Clear tape
- Yarn
- Large sheet of construction paper

Directions: With adult help...

1. Cut out the letters of your first name from pages 31 and 33.

2. Arrange the letters on the 4 ½" x 12" (11.4 cm x 30.5 cm) sheet of construction paper. For names with repeated letters, trace and cut out additional letters to use as stencils.

3. Use just enough glue to hold the letters in place. (You will remove the letters after painting, so just use a little glue.)

4. Dip the end of a sponge painter in paint. Press the sponge painter all over the paper and letters.

5. Place the name hanger on a flat surface. Allow the paint to dry.

6. Carefully remove the stencils from your name hanger.

7. Frame your name hanger by gluing it to the center of a large sheet of construction paper.

8. Tape one end of a piece of yarn on the back upper left corner of the name hanger. Tape the other end of the yarn to the upper right corner.

9. Display your name hanger on the door of your room.

Note: Name hangers make great gifts for friends, so you may want to use the letter stencils more than once. Consider tracing them on a plastic coffee can or margarine lid and cutting them out. These plastic letters can be used again and again.

Directions: Use with the activity on page 30.

Note to the adult: Please cut out the letters in your child's first name.

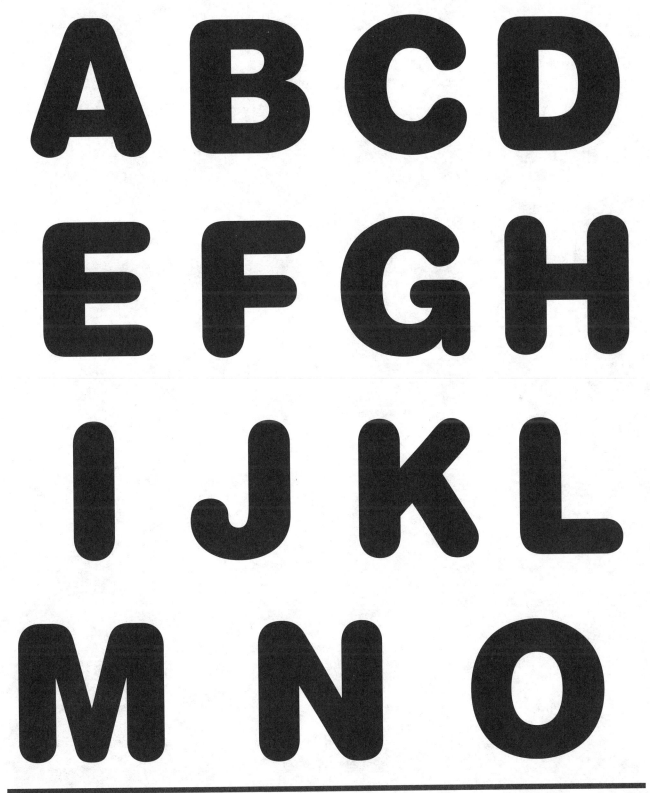

Directions: Use with the activity on page 30.

Note to the adult: Please cut out the letters in your child's first name.

Chalk Rubbings

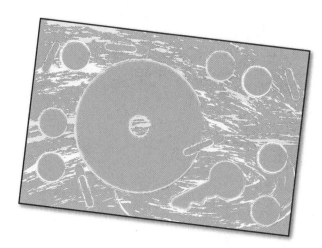

Materials:

- Assortment of flat objects, such as:
  - paper clips
  - coins
  - leaves
  - pine needles
  - buttons
  - combs
  - CDs
  - keys
- Large sheet of paper
- Sidewalk chalk, various colors
- Hairspray (optional)

Directions: With adult help...

1. Select an assortment of objects and lay them on a flat, smooth surface.

2. Cover several objects with a sheet of paper.

3. Hold the chalk on its side. Gently rub the chalk on the paper over the objects.

4. Repeat steps 3 and 4, using different color chalks and objects turned in different directions.

5. If desired, an adult can spray hairspray on the rubbing to help keep the chalk from flaking off the paper.

Safety First! (See page 2.)

Painted Bubble-Saurus

Materials:
- Acrylic or tempera paint
- 8" x 10" (20.3 cm x 25.4 cm) piece of bubble packaging material
- Large paintbrush
- Scissors
- Dinosaur pattern (page 37)
- Crayons or markers

Directions: With adult help...

1. Cut out the dinosaur pattern on page 37.

2. Paint the bubble packaging material using a large paintbrush.

3. Place the Dinosaur pattern on the bubble packaging material. Press down gently.

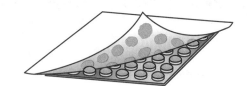

4. Allow the paint on the paper to dry.

5. Use a crayon or marker to add any other details you like.

Dinosaur Pattern

Directions: Use with the activity on page 36.

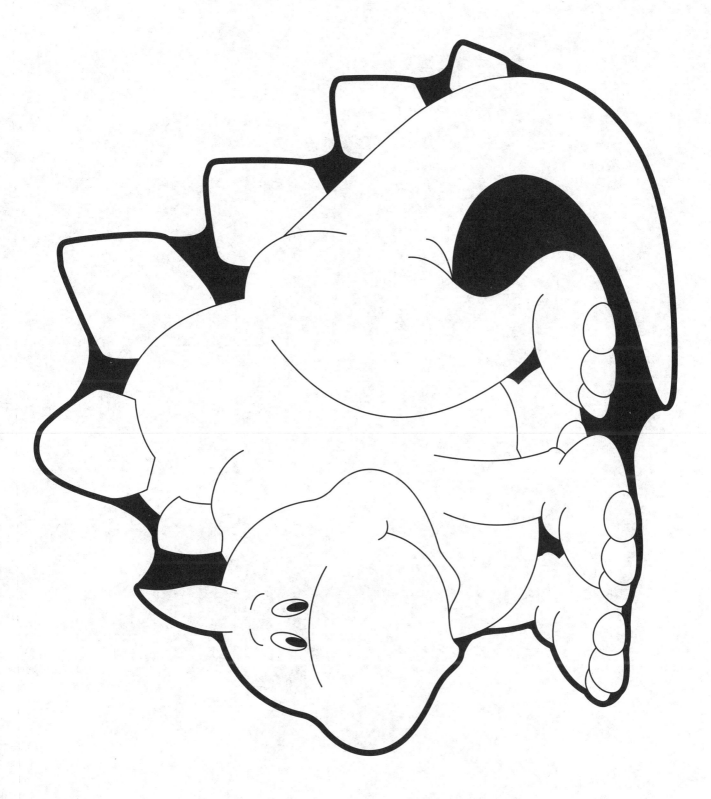

Materials:
- Scissors
- Kazoo cover pattern
- 5" (12.7 cm) cardboard tube (half of a paper towel tube)
- Glue stick
- Hole punch
- 5" (12.7 cm) square of waxed paper
- Rubber band

Directions: With adult help...

1. Cut out the kazoo cover pattern.

2. Cover the outside of the cardboard tube with glue.

3. Wrap the kazoo cover around the tube. Add glue to the overlapping edge. Press it down so that your tube is completely covered.

4. Punch a hole in one end of the kazoo.

5. Cover the other end of the kazoo with waxed paper. Use the rubber band to hold the waxed paper in place.

6. Place your lips inside the open end and hum a tune.

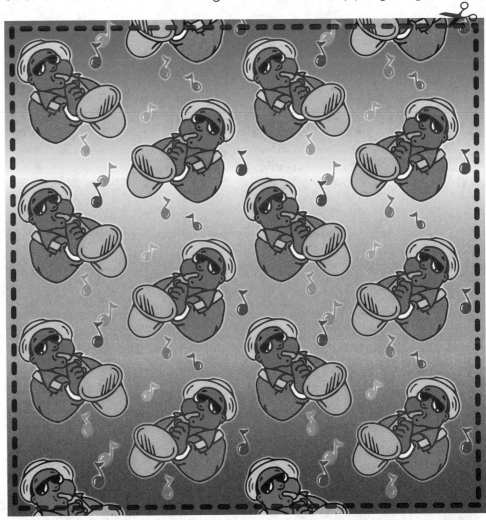

Dancing Rings and Dancing Wands

Materials for Dancing Rings:

- ¼" (0.64 cm) paper ribbon
- Scissors
- Canning jar lid band, plastic bracelet, or 3" (7.6 cm) plastic ring (available in craft supply stores)

Directions for Dancing Rings: With adult help...

1. Cut the ribbon into 10 or more 36" (91 cm) lengths.
2. Tie one end of each ribbon onto the canning jar lid band.
3. To play with the dancing ring, grasp it around the band and dance with large arm movements.

Materials for Dancing Wands:

- ¼" (0.64 cm) paper ribbon
- Scissors
- 4" (10 cm) piece of a wide straw

Directions for Dancing Wands: With adult help...

1. Cut the ribbon into eight 36" (91 cm) lengths.
2. At one end, tie all of the ribbons together in a knot.
3. At the other end, pile all of the ribbons together. Push them through the straw.
4. Tie the ribbons together in pairs so that they do not slip back through the straw.
5. To play with the dancing wand, grasp the straw and dance with large arm movements.

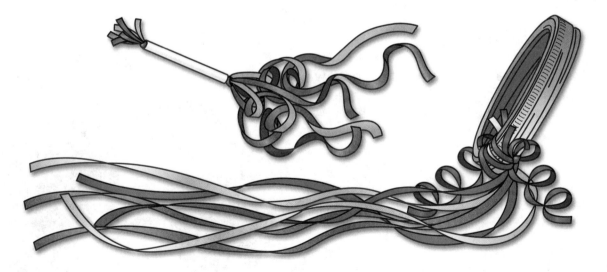

Note: You may want to make two dancing rings or wands so that you can have one in each hand as you move!

Giant Maraca

Materials:
- Pencil
- Two 6"-inch (15.25-cm) diameter paper or disposable foam bowls
- One chenille stem, any color
- Paper ribbon
- ¼ cup of uncooked pasta
- White glue
- Clear tape

Directions: With adult help...

1. Use a pencil to make two holes in the base of one bowl.

2. Thread the chenille stem through both holes so that the ends are inside the bowl.

3. Twist the ends of the chenille stem on the inside. Leave enough of the outside loop to form a handle for your maraca.

4. Make holes about 2" (5 cm) apart around the bowl.

5. Thread lengths of ribbon through the holes from the outside to the inside.

6. Tape the ribbon ends inside the bowl to hold them securely.

7. Cover the rim of one bowl with glue.

8. Place the pasta in the bowl.

9. Carefully match the rims of both bowls. Press them together. Allow the glue to dry completely. Reinforce the edges with tape.

10. To play your maraca, hold the chenille stem handle and shake it gently.

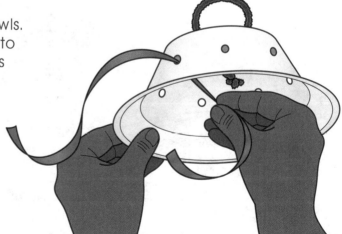

Safety First! (See page 2.)

Materials:
- Two caps from empty 64-oz. juice bottles (approximately 1 ½" [4 cm] diameter)
- White glue
- Sturdy cardboard tube (aluminum foil or plastic wrap tube)
- Aluminum foil
- 1/3 cup of uncooked popcorn or rice
- 2" (5 cm) wide packing tape
- 6" x 18" (15.25 cm x 45.8 cm) brown grocery bag paper or piece of lightweight brown fabric
- Two 8" (20.3 cm) pieces of yarn or ribbon

Directions: With adult help...

1. Cover the inside rim of one juice bottle cap with glue. Place it over one end of the tube. Allow the glue to dry.

2. Tear six squares (approximately 4" [10 cm]) of aluminum foil. Crumple them into balls.

3. Drop the foil balls into the tube.

4. Pour the popcorn kernels or rice into the tube. The pieces should fall easily around the foil and sound like rain. (Adjust the sound by adding or removing a foil ball.)

5. Coat the inside rim of the second juice bottle cap with glue. Place it over the open end of the tube. Allow the glue to dry.

6. Reinforce the caps and tube by wrapping them with packing tape.

7. Put glue along the long edges of the brown paper or fabric.

8. Center the tube on one glued edge. Wrap the paper or fabric around the tube. (It will overlap itself.) Firmly press the edges.

9. Twist the ends of the paper or fabric. Tightly tie the yarn or ribbon close to the tube. Allow the glue to dry thoroughly.

10. To play with the rain stick, gently turn it from end to end and listen to the sound of rain.

 **(See page 2.)**

Materials:
- Two wooden craft sticks
- White glue
- Crayons (red, orange, yellow, green, light blue, dark blue, and purple)
- Seven pieces of paper or disposable foam plate rims, various lengths
- Hole punch
- Five pieces of ribbon or yarn

Directions: With adult help...

1. Make a plus sign with the wooden craft sticks. Glue them at their center. Allow the glue to dry completely.

2. Color each disposable foam plate rim a different color.

3. Punch a hole in one end of each disposable foam plate rim.

4. Tie the center of one ribbon or yarn piece around the glued center of the wooden craft sticks. (This will be the hanger for the mobile.)

5. Tie each end of the remaining ribbon or yarn to a disposable foam plate rim.

6. Tie the disposable foam plate rims to the wooden craft sticks. Secure the ribbon or yarn with a drop of glue.

7. Hang the rainbow mobile where everyone in your family will enjoy it.

Paper Plate Fish

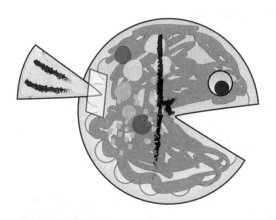

Materials:
- Scissors
- 8" (20.3 cm) paper plate
- Glue (or tape or a stapler)
- Crayons, paint, or markers
- Googly eyes (optional)
- Sequins, glitter, or glitter glue (optional)

Directions: With adult help...

1. Cut a wedge out of a paper plate. The wedge will be the fish's tail. The hole that the wedge leaves will be the fish's mouth.

2. Glue (or tape or staple) the tail to the opposite side of the plate from the mouth.

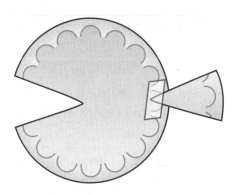

3. Color the fish.

4. Glue a googly eye on the fish or simply draw an eye.

5. Decorate your fish with glitter, glitter glue, or sequins.

Paper Plate Ladybug

Materials:
- Red tempera paint
- Paintbrush
- Two 6" (15.25 cm) paper plates
- Black marker
- Scissors
- Hole punch (optional)
- Red chenille stem
- Two brass paper fasteners

Directions: With adult help...

1. Paint both plates with red paint. (If desired, paint both sides of the plates.) Allow the paint to dry.

2. Use the marker to draw black spots on both plates.

3. Cut one plate in half. These pieces will be the wings. The other plate will be the body.

4. Lay one wing on the body. Punch a hole through the body and the wing near the corner of the wing. Put the wing aside.

5. Lay the other wing on the body. Punch a hole through this wing and the body. Put the wing aside.

6. Fold the chenille stem in half. Push one end up through each hole in the ladybug's body. Twist the chenille stem once so that it stands up by itself.

7. Thread the wings onto the chenille stem so that they lay flat on the ladybug.

8. Push one brass paper fastener down through each hole. Open the wings of the fasteners under the ladybug.

9. Curl the ends of the chenille stem to resemble antennae.

Safari Hat

Materials:
- Scissors
- 8" (20.3 cm) paper or disposable foam plate
- White glue
- 6" (15.2 cm) paper or disposable foam bowl
- Tempera paint (olive green or tan)
- Animal pictures (below)
- 22" (56 cm) of cord or thick yarn
- Two 14" (36 cm) pieces of cord or thick yarn

Directions: With adult help...

1. Cut out a 5" (12.7 cm) diameter circle in the center of a paper or disposable foam plate. (This will be the brim of the hat.)

2. Turn the plate circle upside-down.

3. Glue a paper or disposable foam bowl to the plate circle to form the hat. Allow the glue to dry.

4. Paint the hat inside and outside. Allow the paint to dry.

5. Cut out the animal pictures.

6. Glue the pictures around the top of the hat.

7. Glue the 22" (56 cm) piece of cord or yarn around the hat.

8. Make a hole in each side of the hat's brim.

9. Tie one piece of 14" (36 cm) cord in each hole. Use the cords to hold the safari hat on your head.

Gardener's Hat

Materials:
* Scissors
* 8" (20.3 cm) disposable foam plate
* White glue
* 6" (15.2 cm) disposable foam bowl
* Tempera paint (any bright color)
* Garden tool pictures (below)
* 22" (56 cm) of ribbon or lace
* Two 14" (36 cm) pieces of ribbon

Directions: With adult help...

1. Cut out a 5" (12.7 cm) diameter circle in the center of a paper or disposable foam plate. (This will be the brim of the hat.)

2. Turn the plate circle upside-down.

3. Glue a paper or disposable foam bowl to the plate circle to form the hat. Allow the glue to dry.

4. Paint the hat inside and outside. Allow the paint to dry.

5. Cut out the garden tool pictures.

6. Glue the pictures around the top of the hat.

7. Glue the 22" (56 cm) piece of ribbon or lace around the hat.

8. Make a hole in each side of the hat's brim.

9. Tie one piece of 14" (36 cm) ribbon in each hole. Use the cords to hold the gardener's hat on your head.

49

Easy-to-Make Dough

Use the recipes on pages 51–53 to make materials for the dough sculptures on pages 54–56.

Ingredients:
- 1 cup cornstarch
- 1 ½ cups flour
- Warm water

Utensils:
- Large mixing bowl
- Measuring cup
- Wooden mixing spoon

Directions: With adult help…

1. Add the cornstarch to the flour in a large bowl. Mix well.
2. Add warm water a little at a time. Mix to make a stiff dough.
3. To handle the dough, dust your hands and the dough with a little flour to prevent sticking.
4. Play with the dough like modeling clay. The shapes and sculptures you make will dry in two or three days and can be painted.

Safety First! (See page 2.)

"The Best" Play Dough

Use the recipes on pages 51–53 to make materials for the dough sculptures on pages 54–56.

Ingredients:
- Food coloring (optional)
- 1 cup salt
- 2 cups sifted flour
- 2 tablespoons alum (found with spices in the grocery store)
- 2 tablespoons vegetable oil
- 1 cup water

Utensils:
- Large bowl
- Measuring cups and spoons
- Wooden mixing spoon

Directions: With adult help...
1. If colored dough is desired, add three or four drops of food coloring to the water. If not, go to step 2.
2. Mix all of the ingredients together with your hands or the mixing spoon until a smooth dough is formed.
3. If stored in an airtight container, the dough will keep for several weeks.

 **(See page 2.)**

Use the recipes on pages 51–53 to make materials for the dough sculptures on pages 54–56.

Ingredients:
- 2 ½ cups boiling water
- 1 cup cornstarch
- ½ cup cold water

Utensils:
- Large microwave-safe bowl
- Measuring cup
- Plastic jar with tight-fitting lid (clean mayonnaise jars work well)
- Wooden mixing spoon

Directions: With adult help…

1. Microwave 2 ½ cups of water to the boiling point.
2. While the water is heating, mix 1 cup of cornstarch with ½ cup cold water in a large plastic jar. (Or, you can mix them in a small bowl.)
3. Carefully remove the hot water from the microwave.
4. Add the cornstarch mixture to the hot water. Stir constantly until the consistency is like clay.
5. Play with the cool dough like modeling clay. The shapes and sculptures you make will dry at room temperature. After 36 hours, the clay will become very hard. It can be painted and sprayed with shellac.

 **(See page 2.)**

Materials for all projects:
• Supply of homemade or purchased play dough.

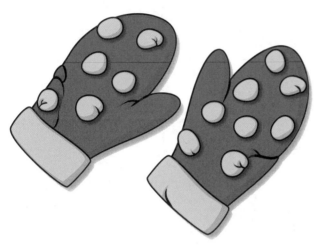

Mittens

Use the picture to help you make the mittens. Decorate your mittens anyway you like.

Snowman

Use the picture to help you make the snowman. Add little pieces of dough for eyes, a nose, a mouth, and buttons if you like.

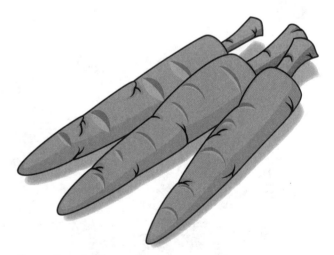

Bunch of Grapes

Use the picture to help you make the grapes. Be sure to add stems.

Bunch of Carrots

Use the picture to help you make the carrots. Make shallow cuts in the carrots to give them some texture.

Dough Sculptures

Materials for all projects:
- Supply of homemade or purchased play dough.

Turtle

Use the picture to help you make the turtle. Don't forget to give him a tail!

Jellyfish

Use the picture to help you make the jellyfish. He's friendly, so add a smile and eyes!

Bunny

Use the picture to help you make the bunny. Did you notice she's made with ovals and circles?

Dough Sculptures

Materials for all projects:
- Supply of homemade or purchased play dough.

Bear

Use the picture to help you make the bear. He's made with circles and ovals too!

Tractor

Use the picture to help you make the tractor. What shapes do you see?

Dump Truck

Use the picture to help you make the dump truck. What shapes make up the dump truck?

Caterpillar

Materials:
- Clothespin
- White glue
- Scissors
- One brown or black chenille stem
- Five small green pom-poms
- Two whole cloves, tiny black pom-poms, or bits of black felt
- 1" (2.5 cm) length of magnetic strip tape

Directions: With adult help…

1. Place the clothespin on a flat surface so that it opens in an up and down direction.

2. Cover the top of the clothespin with a thick layer of glue.

3. Cut short pieces of a chenille stem. Place the pieces in the glue on the clothespin about ½" (1.25 cm) apart to make the legs of the caterpillar.

4. Place five small pom-poms touching each other in the glue. Allow the glue to dry.

5. Bend the caterpillar legs down on both sides of the clothespin.

6. Bend a short chenille stem piece into a V shape to make the caterpillar's antennae. Glue it between the first and second pom-pom.

7. Make eyes with whole cloves, tiny pom-poms, or small bits of felt.

8. Secure the magnetic strip to the back of the clothespin.

9. Display your critter magnet on the refrigerator.

Safety First! (See page 2.)

Duck

Materials:
- White glue
- One small and one medium yellow pom-pom
- Yellow feathers
- Orange felt scraps
- Two whole cloves, tiny black pom-poms, or bits of black felt
- Clothespin
- 1" (2.5 cm) length of magnetic strip tape

Directions: With adult help...

1. Glue the pom-poms together to make the duck's head and body.

2. Glue a yellow feather on the medium pom-pom for the duck's tail.

3. Glue one yellow feather on each side of the medium pom-pom to make the wings.

4. Cut heart shapes from orange felt to make feet for the duck.

5. Make a beak with a scrap of orange felt.

6. Make eyes with whole cloves, tiny pom-poms, or small bits of felt.

7. Glue the duck to the clothespin.

8. Secure the magnetic strip to the back of the clothespin.

9. Display your critter magnet on the refrigerator.

 Safety First! (See page 2.)

Flamingo

Materials:
- Two large, one medium, and one small pink pom-poms
- Pink feathers
- Clothespin
- White glue
- One 6" (15.25 cm) pink chenille stem
- Two whole cloves, tiny black pom-poms, or bits of black felt

Directions: With adult help…

1. Glue the two large, one medium, and one small pink pom-poms together in a row in that order. Allow the glue to dry.

2. Glue pink feathers onto the pom-poms. Allow the glue to dry.

3. Cover the top of the clothespin with a thick layer of glue.

4. Bend a 6" (15.25 cm) pink chenille stem in half. Place the strip at the middle of the clothespin just above the metal spring. (A slight indentation is at this spot on the clothespin.) Press the chenille stem flat.

5. Press the feather-covered pom-pom flamingo body into the glue on the clothespin. Allow the glue to dry completely.

6. Make a beak and eyes with whole cloves, tiny pom-poms, or small bits of felt.

7. Enjoy your critter!

Red Bird

Materials:
- White glue
- One small and one medium red pom-pom
- Red feathers
- Two whole cloves, tiny black pom-poms, or bits of black felt
- Clothespin
- 1" (2.5 cm) length of magnetic strip tape

Directions: With adult help...

1. Glue the pom-poms together to make the red bird's head and body.
2. Glue a red feather on the medium pom-pom for the red bird's tail.
3. Glue one red feather on each side of the medium pom-pom to make the wings.
4. Make a beak and eyes with whole cloves, tiny pom-poms, or small bits of felt.
5. Glue the bird to the clothespin.
6. Secure the magnetic strip to the back of the clothespin.
7. Display your critter magnet on the refrigerator.

Butterfly

Safety First! (See page 2.)

Materials:
- Scissors
- Three orange chenille stems
- Clothespin
- White glue
- Four small yellow pom-poms
- 1" (2.5 cm) length of magnetic strip tape

Directions: With adult help...

1. Cut two 8" (20.3 cm) pieces of chenille stem. Bend each piece into a wide loop. Twist the ends together to make the large front wings.
2. Cut two 6" (15.25 cm) pieces of chenille stem. Bend each piece into a wide loop. Twist the ends together to make the smaller back wings.
3. Cover the top of the clothespin with a thick layer of glue.
4. Place the pom-poms almost touching each other in the glue.
5. Place the large front wings in the glue between the first two pom-poms.
6. Place the smaller wings in the glue between the last two pom-poms. Allow the glue to dry.
7. Cut a small piece from a chenille stem. Bend it in half.
8. Curl the tips. Glue it behind the head of the butterfly for antennae.
9. Secure the magnetic strip to the back of the clothespin.
10. Display your critter magnet on the refrigerator.

Button Pin

Materials:
- Waxed paper
- 2" x 5" (5 cm x 12.7 cm) piece lightweight cardboard
- 12 to 14 small buttons (¼"–½" [0.64 cm to 1.25 cm])
- White glue
- ½" to 1" (1.25 cm to 2.5 cm) jewelry bar pin

Directions: With adult help…

1. Cover your work surface with waxed paper. (This will protect it from the glue and make the project easier to remove when the glue dries.)
2. Glue four or five buttons face-up and touching in a row to the cardboard.
3. Glue three or four buttons on top of the first layer. Stagger their placement over the places where the first buttons touch.
4. Glue two or three buttons on top of the second layer. Stagger their placement over the second row.
5. Glue one or two buttons on top. Allow the glue to dry completely.
6. Gently peel away the waxed paper.
7. Glue a jewelry bar pin to the back.

Safety First! (See page 2.)

Puzzle Pin

Materials:
- Waxed paper
- 6 to 8 small (1"–1 ½" [2.5 cm to 3.8 cm]) jigsaw puzzle pieces (This is a good way to recycle old puzzles that already have missing pieces.)
- White glue
- ½" to 1" (1.25 cm to 2.5 cm) jewelry bar pin

Directions: With adult help…

1. Cover your work surface with waxed paper. (This will protect it from the glue and make the project easier to remove when the glue dries.)
2. Glue three or four puzzle pieces face-up and touching in a row.
3. Glue two or three puzzle pieces on top of the first layer. Stagger their placement over the places where the first puzzle pieces touch.
4. Glue another layer of pieces on top of the second layer. Stagger their placement over the second row.
5. Allow the glue to dry completely. Gently pull the project away from the waxed paper.
6. Glue a jewelry bar pin to the back.

Feather Pin

Materials:
- Waxed paper
- Large button
- Scrap of cardboard
- Pencil
- White glue
- 6 to 8 craft feathers, any color
- ½" to 1" (1.25 cm to 2.5 cm) jewelry bar pin

Directions: With adult help...

1. Cover your work surface with waxed paper. (This will protect it from the glue and make the project easier to remove when the glue dries.)
2. Place a ½" to ¾" (1.25 cm to 1.9 cm) button in the center of the cardboard.
3. Trace around the button.
4. Remove the button. Glue five or six craft feathers around the tracing. Place the feathers so that their tips are inside the drawn button.
5. Glue the button in the center of the feathers.
6. Allow the glue to dry completely. Gently pull the project away from the waxed paper.
7. Glue a jewelry bar pin to the back.

 **Safety First!** (See page 2.)

Posey Pin

Materials:
- Waxed paper
- One green chenille stem
- One pop-pom
- White glue
- Two yellow chenille stems
- ½" to 1" (1.25 cm to 2.5 cm) jewelry bar pin

Directions: With adult help...

1. Cover your work surface with waxed paper. (This will protect it from the glue and make the project easier to remove when the glue dries.)
2. Bend each yellow chenille stem into the shape of an eight.
3. Put the two yellow stems together in the middle. Wrap the center with the green chenille stem.
4. Bend the rest of the green chenille stem into a flower stem and one or two leaves.
5. Glue the pom-pom in the middle of the flower.
6. Allow the glue to dry. Gently pull the project away from the waxed paper.
7. Glue a jewelry bar pin to the back.

Raccoon Mask

Materials:
- Scissors
- Raccoon Face and Ear Piece Patterns (page 65)
- Raccoon Mask, Ears, Nose, and Mouth Patterns (page 67)
- White glue
- Stapler
- Clear tape

Directions: With adult help…

1. Cut out the Raccoon Face and Ear Piece Patterns (page 65).

2. Cut out the Raccoon Mask, Ears, Nose, and Mouth Patterns (page 67).

3. Glue the mask in the center of the face.

4. Fold the ear pieces in half. Glue them together. (This will make them stronger.)

5. Staple one ear piece to each side of the face. Cover the staples with tape to prevent scratching.

6. Glue the edge of each ear. Press it to the back of the face over the eyes.

7. Glue the nose to the mouth piece. Glue the mouth piece in the center of the face under the mask.

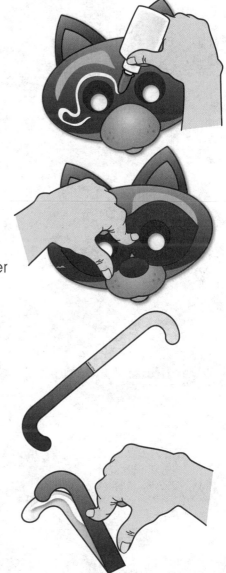

Raccoon Face and Ear Piece Patterns

Directions: Use with the activity on page 63.

Note to the adult: Make sure to cut out the eye circles on the face piece.

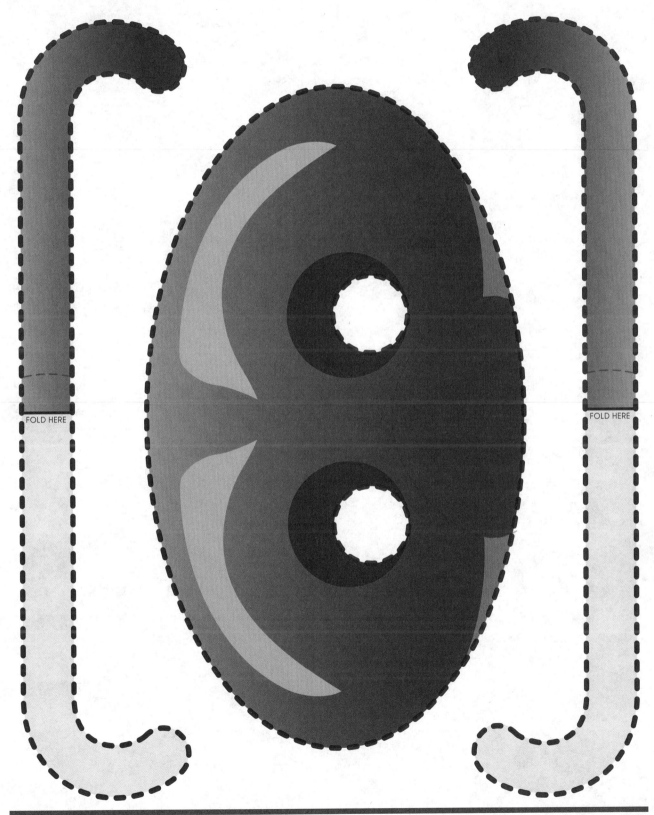

FOLD HERE

FOLD HERE

⸺ Raccoon Mask, Ears, Nose, and Mouth Patterns ⸺

Directions: Use with the activity on page 63.

Note to the adult: Make sure to cut out the eye circles on the mask piece.

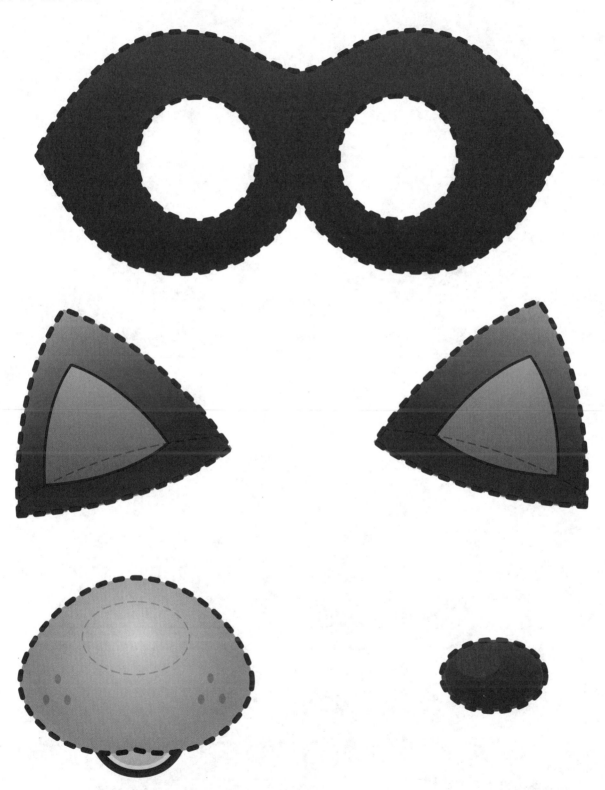

Elephant Mask

Materials:
- Scissors
- Elephant Face, Trunk, and Ear Patterns (page 71)
- Elephant Mask and Ear Piece Patterns (page 73)
- White glue
- Stapler
- Clear tape

Directions: With adult help...

1. Cut out the Elephant Face, Trunk, and Ear Patterns (page 71).

2. Cut out the Elephant Mask and Ear Piece Patterns (page 73).

3. Glue the face in the center of the mask.

4. Glue one ear on each side of the mask.

5. Fold the ear pieces in half. Glue them together. (This will make them stronger.)

6. Staple one ear piece to each side of the mask behind the elephant's ears. Cover the staples with tape to prevent scratching.

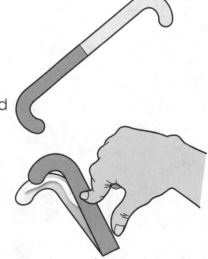

7. Fold the trunk back and forth accordion style.

8. Glue the trunk in the center of the face between the elephant's eyes.

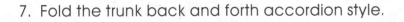

Elephant Face, Trunk, and Ear Patterns

Directions: Use with the activity on page 69.

Note to the adult: Make sure to cut out the eye circles on the face piece.

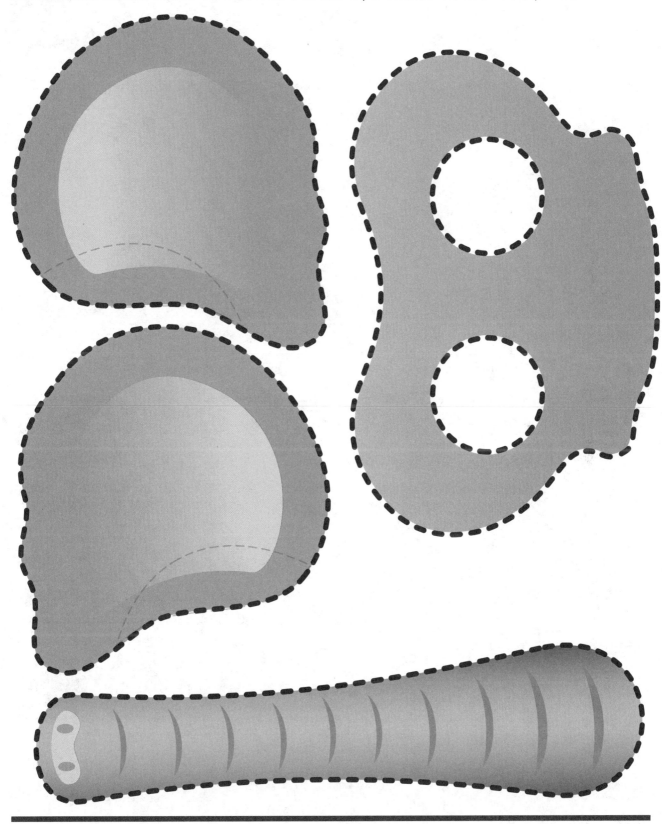

Elephant Mask and Ear Piece Patterns

Directions: Use with the activity on page 69.

Note to the adult: Make sure to cut out the eye circles on the mask piece.

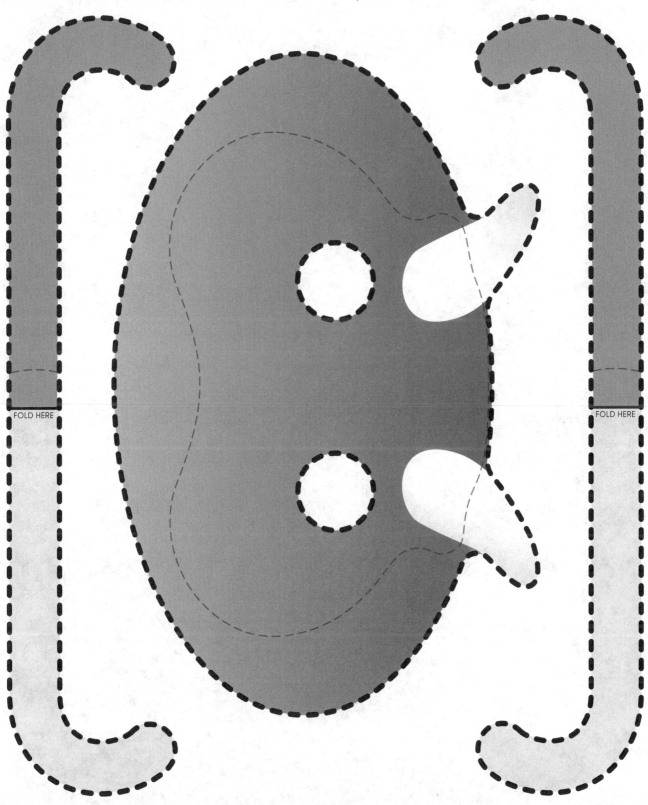

FOLD HERE

FOLD HERE

Materials:
- Scissors
- Lion Face, Mane, Ears, and Nose Patterns (page 77)
- Lion Mask and Ear Piece Patterns (page 79)
- Yellow or light brown construction paper
- Pencil
- Glue stick
- Stapler
- Tape
- Marker (black or brown)

Directions: With adult help...

1. Cut out the Lion Face, Mane, Ears, and Nose Patterns (page 77).

2. Cut out the Lion Mask and Ear Piece Patterns (page 79).

3. Fold a sheet of yellow or light brown construction paper in half. Fold it in half again.

4. Put the mane pattern on the folded paper as shown. Trace the pattern.

5. Cut out the mane along the traced lines.

6. Make shallow cuts (approximately 1 ¼" [3.2 cm]) toward the center all of the way around the mane.

7. Glue the mask on top of the mane.

8. Glue the face in mask's center, matching the holes for the eyes.

9. Fold the ear pieces in half. Glue them together. (This will make them stronger.)

10. Staple one ear piece to each side of the mask. Cover the staples with tape to prevent scratching.

11. Glue the edge of each ear. Press them to the mask over the eyes.

12. Glue the nose in the center of the face.

13. Draw a mouth for the lion with a marker.

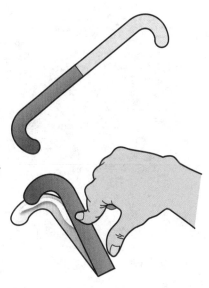

Lion Face, Mane, Ears, and Nose Patterns

Directions: Use with the activity on page 75.

Note to the adult: Make sure to cut out the eye circles on the face piece.

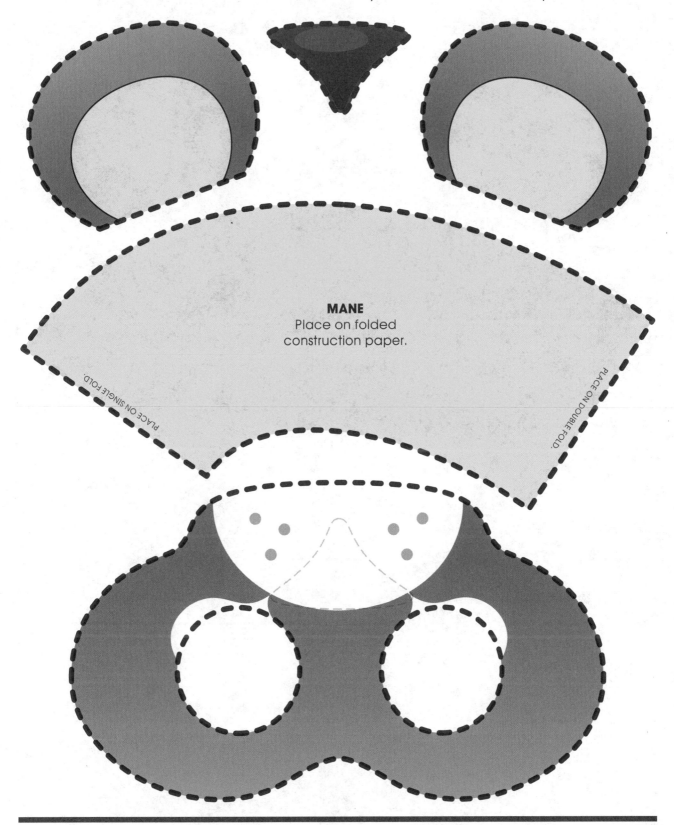

MANE
Place on folded
construction paper.

PLACE ON SINGLE FOLD.

PLACE ON DOUBLE FOLD.

Lion Mask and Ear Piece Patterns

Directions: Use with the activity on page 75.

Note to the adult: Make sure to cut out the eye circles on the mask piece.

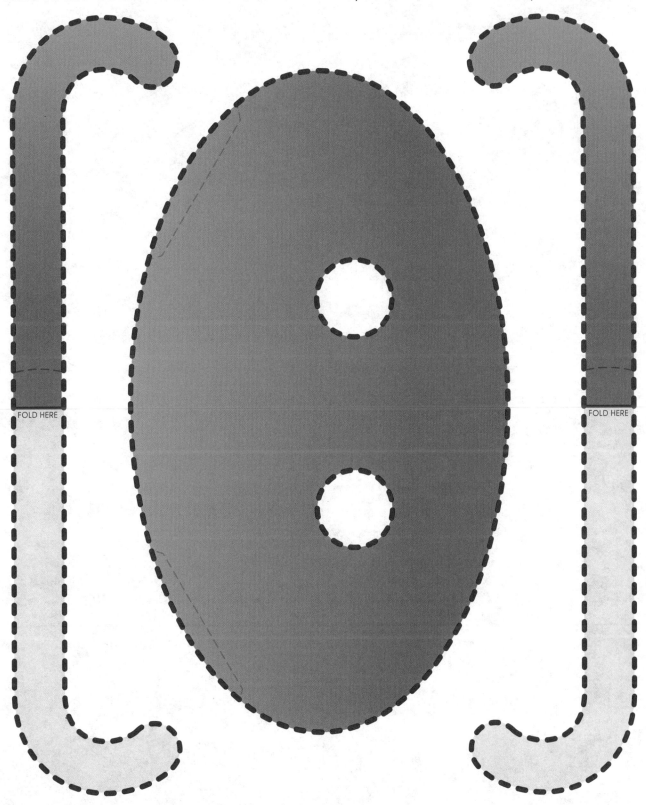

FOLD HERE

FOLD HERE